DESERT TREE FINDER

A Pocket Manual for Identifying Desert Trees

MAY THEILGAARD WATTS and TOM WATTS

Nature Study
Guild Publishers
an imprint of AdventureKEEN

To identify a tree, begin on the next page
with the first choice:

either or

. . . and go on from there. After a few
more choices, you'll come to a drawing
and the name of your tree.

advice: See pages 2–7 before you begin

Approximate area covered by this book

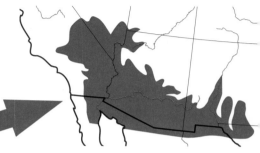

This book is for identifying trees of the desert and dry desert hills, and some
trees commonly grown in human-made oases. For higher altitudes that have
enough rainfall for pine trees, use:
the ROCKY MOUNTAIN TREE FINDER (Arizona, New Mexico)
the PACIFIC COAST TREE FINDER (California)

You can tell pine trees by their long
needles bundled together at the base:

© 2024 Keen Communications; © 1974 Nature Study Guild • ISBN 978-0-912550-48-0 • Printed in China •
Cataloging-in-Publication data is available from the Library of Congress • naturestudy.com

BEGIN HERE

If the tree you are identifying grows among:

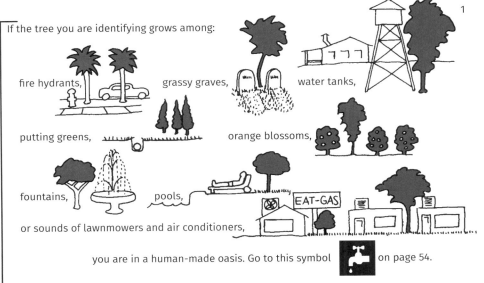

fire hydrants,

grassy graves,

water tanks,

putting greens,

orange blossoms,

fountains,

pools,

or sounds of lawnmowers and air conditioners,

you are in a human-made oasis. Go to this symbol on page 54.

If there is no water supply in pipes or ditches, go to this symbol on page 8.

Maps in this book show the natural ranges of trees. ⟶

These symbols show how or where desert trees are likely to grow:

 Riparian trees—their roots are in permanent underground water.

Trees of desert washes—they grow where flood waters gather after a thunderstorm.

Evergreen trees are in leaf all year long.

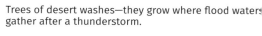 Trees leafless in dry seasons—they leaf out only after a good rain.

 Trees are leafless in winter only.

Trees of the oak-juniper woodland. These trees of higher altitudes also grow in canyons and cool slopes at the edge of the desert.

 Trees introduced by humans and that have escaped from cultivation and are now growing wild

 Domesticated trees of the desert, planted in parks, yards, and cemeteries

 Trees considered invasive in some areas

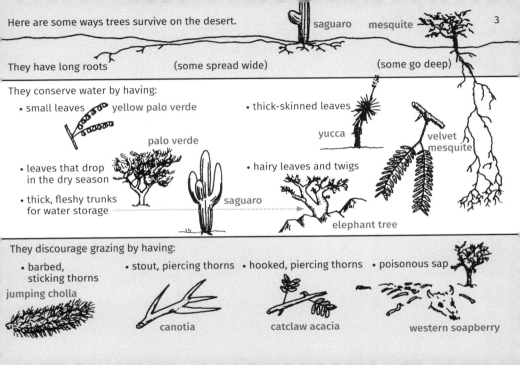

Here are some ways trees survive on the desert.

saguaro   mesquite

They have long roots   (some spread wide)   (some go deep)

They conserve water by having:

- small leaves   yellow palo verde

palo verde

- leaves that drop in the dry season
- thick, fleshy trunks for water storage   saguaro

- thick-skinned leaves

yucca   velvet mesquite

- hairy leaves and twigs

elephant tree

They discourage grazing by having:

- barbed, sticking thorns   • stout, piercing thorns   • hooked, piercing thorns   • poisonous sap

jumping cholla

canotia   catclaw acacia   western soapberry

RAINFALL Most of the rain in the desert region falls in the cool higher altitudes of the surrounding mountains. Lower altitudes are warmer, but the rainfall there may dry up in midair. The high-rainfall areas on this map show also where the high mountains are:

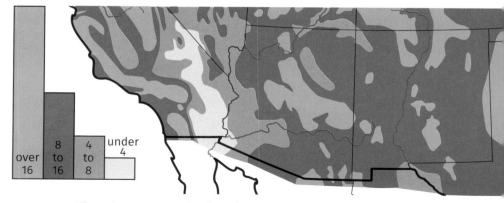

Where the average yearly rainfall is less than 16 inches, it makes a great difference to tree how much the amount of rain varies from year to year, and what season the rain falls mat which is dependent on seasonal winds from the Atlantic and Pacific Oceans.

Winter Rain

Weakened remnants of the winter storms that drench the California coast can bring sparse, gentle rain east as far as the Continental Divide. But many desert trees can't benefit from rain in winter, when it's too cold for their roots to grow or seeds to germinate. Winter rains seldom reach the Chihuahuan Desert. It has dry, frosty winters.

Summer Rain

Monsoon winds can bring unstable tropical air from the Gulf of Mexico. The resulting thunder showers soak unevenly into the soil, but they come at the best season for trees. Summer rains are most reliable in the eastern end of the Sonoran Desert (the desert with the most abundant trees). To the west, the rains thin out and may even skip a year. The trees are smaller and farther apart too.

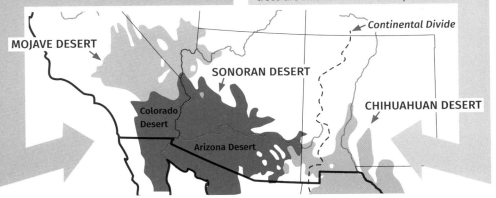

DESERT SOILS

Desert mountains stand knee-deep in their own debris—eroded rock, gravel, sand, and clay—which forms long bajadas (slopes) leading down to an intermountain basin or valley. In the desert dryness, soil changes along these slopes can mean life or death for trees. Violent, splashing rain causes sheet erosion, which makes a network of temporary watercourses emptying into desert washes. The erosion carries the finer soil particles farther downslope

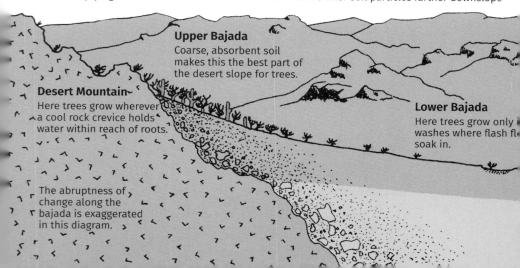

Upper Bajada
Coarse, absorbent soil makes this the best part of the desert slope for trees.

Desert Mountain
Here trees grow wherever a cool rock crevice holds water within reach of roots.

Lower Bajada
Here trees grow only i washes where flash fl soak in.

The abruptness of change along the bajada is exaggerated in this diagram.

than the coarser sand and gravel. So as you descend a bajada, the trees thin out because soils become finer, less porous, and less able to absorb the quick rains that run off and collect in the washes. Trees grow in the washes, especially where a layer of windblown sand collects in the depressions and holds moisture in the soil.

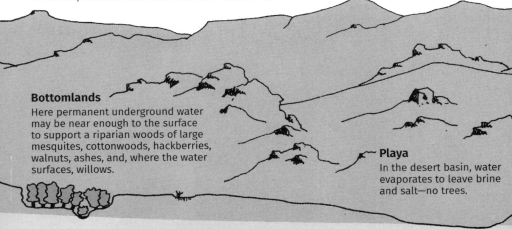

Bottomlands
Here permanent underground water may be near enough to the surface to support a riparian woods of large mesquites, cottonwoods, hackberries, walnuts, ashes, and, where the water surfaces, willows.

Playa
In the desert basin, water evaporates to leave brine and salt—no trees.

level of permanent underground water

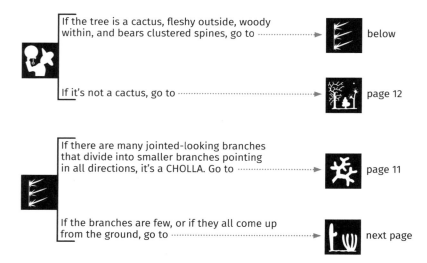

If the tree is a cactus, fleshy outside, woody within, and bears clustered spines, go to below

If it's not a cactus, go to page 12

If there are many jointed-looking branches that divide into smaller branches pointing in all directions, it's a CHOLLA. Go to page 11

If the branches are few, or if they all come up from the ground, go to next page

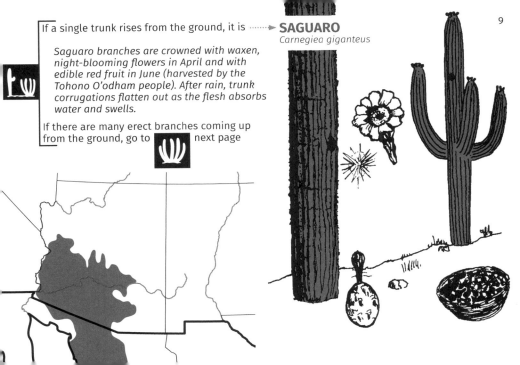

If a single trunk rises from the ground, it is ┄┄┄▶ **SAGUARO**
Carnegiea giganteus

Saguaro branches are crowned with waxen, night-blooming flowers in April and with edible red fruit in June (harvested by the Tohono O'odham people). After rain, trunk corrugations flatten out as the flesh absorbs water and swells.

If there are many erect branches coming up from the ground, go to next page

9

If the upper parts of the branches are bearded with gray, twisted spines, it is ·····➤ **SENITA**
Pachycereus schottii

Senita branches are crowned April to August with pink, night-blooming flowers, and later with small, red fruits eaten by cattle. It's rare in the US.

If the branches aren't bearded, it is ·········➤ **ORGANPIPE CACTUS**
Stenocereus thurberi

From May to June there are creamy-white flowers; later, its many juicy, sweet, red fruits are harvested by the Tohono O'odham people.

If the jointed branches are densely covered with straw-colored spines, the trunk bark is black, and the fruits dangle in long clusters, it is ·····> **JUMPING CHOLLA**
Cylindropuntia fulgida

The joints, which can sprout a new plant, detach or "jump" at a touch. Barbed spines discourage a second touch.

If the spines are dark, of uneven length, and the trunk bark is lighter, it is ·····> **STAGHORN CHOLLA**
Cylindropuntia versicolor

Flowers are orange to brown. Fruit persists on the plant through the winter.

If all leaves are clustered at the tip of a single trunk, or at the tips of the branches, go to ········► below

If they are not so clustered, or if the tree is leafless, go to ··········► page 16

If the leaves are long-stemmed and fan-shaped, it is ·····················► **CALIFORNIA FAN PALM**
Washingtonia filifera

If the leaves are stemless and spear-shaped, it's a YUCCA. Go to ··········► next page

If the tree has many branches; and if there are small, sharp teeth along the leaf edges, it is ··············▶ **JOSHUA TREE**
Yucca brevifolia

If there are only a few branches, or just a main trunk; and if the leaves are edged with peeling fibers, go to ·······▶ next page

If the leaves are flexible, grasslike,
it is ·········➤ **SOAPTREE YUCCA PALMILLA**
Yucca elata

*The flower stalk is long, bearing many
flowers on its upper part, but naked on
its lower part. Seed capsules open in
three parts to release seeds, then remain
on the stalk through the winter.*

If the leaves are stiff, daggerlike; and dead
leaves cover the trunk almost to its base,
go to ·········➤ next page

On dry yucca seedpods you'll find a small
hole made by the escape of a larva that
fed on some of the seeds. It grew from an
egg laid by a female yucca moth, whose
instinct then made her pollinate the yucca
flower, thereby ensuring seed formation.
This probably happened at night, when
desert creatures do business after hiding
from the hot daytime sun.

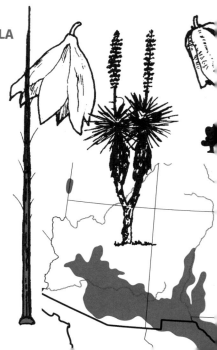

If the leaf is edged with coarse, splinter-like fibers and the flower cluster is shorter, it is ·····➤ **MOJAVE YUCCA**
Yucca schidigera

If the leaf has many whitish threads along its edge and flower clusters are 3–4 feet long, it is ·····➤ **TORREY YUCCA**
Yucca treculeana

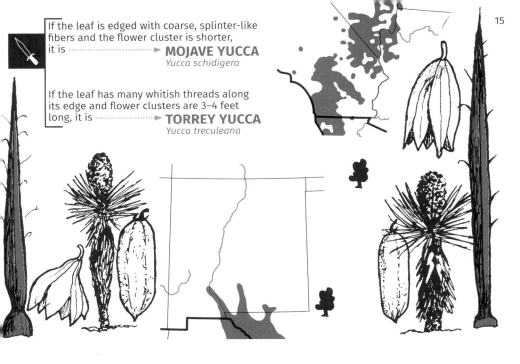

16

If the tree has green or gray twigs ending in sharp, tapered thorns or spines; and the leaves are either totally absent, or else small, ephemeral, and unimportant, go to below

In winter, or the dry season, you may have to look under the tree for its leaves.

If there are thorns or spines along the side of the twig rather than just at the end; or if there are some leaves big enough for a fly to hide under; or if there are just leaves without any thorns at all, go to page 21

If almost the whole tree has smooth, yellow-green bark; or if there are yellow flowers, bean-like pods, or tiny compound leaves, it is

If the tree isn't like that, go to page 18

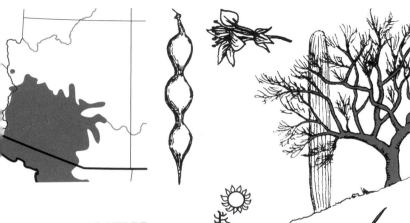

YELLOW PALO VERDE
FOOTHILL PALO VERDE
Parkinsonia microphylla

This tree is usually the one providing the shade required for the growth of saguaro cactus seedlings. It can shed branches in drought.

If the tree looks like a cloud of gray smoke in the distance because of the gray-green twigs, and if the twigs are marked with many brownish gland dots, it is ····▶ **SMOKETHORN**
Psorothamnus spionsus

This tree grows only in frost-free desert washes. In early summer, it's wrapped in a blue veil of indigo flowers.

If the tree isn't like that, go to next page

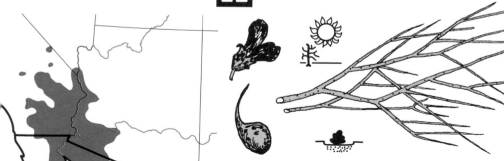

If the branches grow at a wide angle (almost a right angle), or if there are dark berries, it is ·············▶ **ALLTHORN**
CRUCIFIXION THORN
Koeberlinia spinosa

You'll find bad-smelling flowers March to June.

If the branches grow at a narrower angle, forming broomlike masses, go to next page

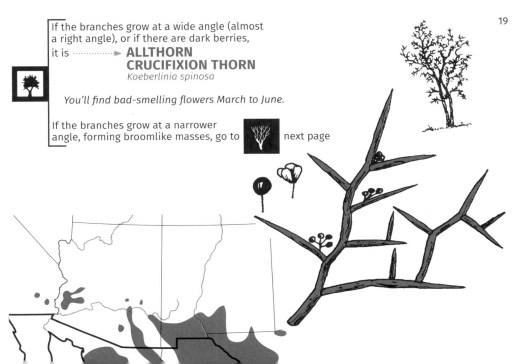

If the twigs are stiff, hairy when young, and there are old black fruits hanging on for years,
it is ········► **HOLACANTHA CRUCIFIXION THORN**
Castela emoryi

If the twigs are flexible; bark smooth and green, but rough near the trunk base; and the fruit is a hard, egg-shaped capsule that splits open,
it is ········► **CANOTIA CRUCIFIXION THORN**
Canotia holacantha

This is the most common of the three crucifixion thorns.

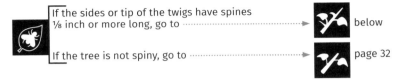

If the sides or tip of the twigs have spines ⅛ inch or more long, go to ⟶ below

If the tree is not spiny, go to ⟶ page 32

If the tree has pods, a wide-spreading top, clustered flowers, and compound leaves (composed of many small leaflets), go to ⟶ page 24

If it's not like that, go to ⟶ next page

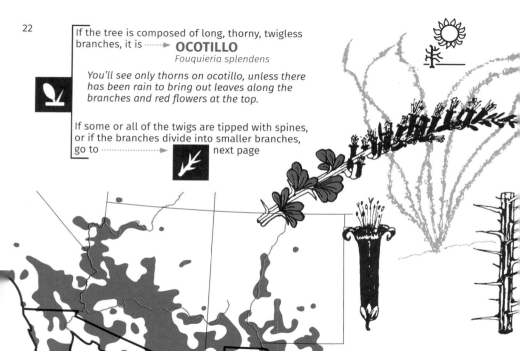

If the tree is composed of long, thorny, twigless branches, it is ·······▶ **OCOTILLO**
Fouquieria splendens

You'll see only thorns on ocotillo, unless there has been rain to bring out leaves along the branches and red flowers at the top.

If some or all of the twigs are tipped with spines, or if the branches divide into smaller branches, go to ··················▶ next page

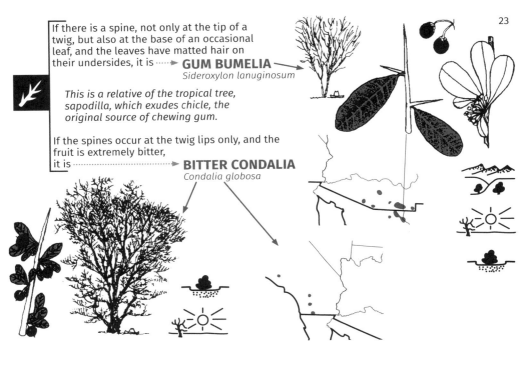

If there is a spine, not only at the tip of a twig, but also at the base of an occasional leaf, and the leaves have matted hair on their undersides, it is ⋯⋯ **GUM BUMELIA**
Sideroxylon lanuginosum

This is a relative of the tropical tree, sapodilla, which exudes chicle, the original source of chewing gum.

If the spines occur at the twig tips only, and the fruit is extremely bitter, it is ⋯⋯⋯⋯⋯⋯⋯⋯ **BITTER CONDALIA**
Condalia globosa

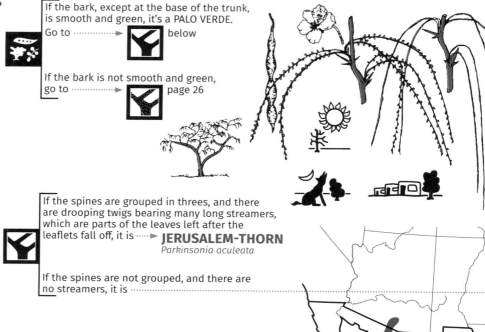

If the bark, except at the base of the trunk, is smooth and green, it's a PALO VERDE.

Go to ┈┈┈► ▼ below

If the bark is not smooth and green, go to ┈┈┈► ▼ page 26

If the spines are grouped in threes, and there are drooping twigs bearing many long streamers, which are parts of the leaves left after the leaflets fall off, it is ┈┈┈► **JERUSALEM-THORN**
Parkinsonia aculeata

If the spines are not grouped, and there are no streamers, it is ┈┈┈┈┈┈┈┈┈┈┈┈┈┈┈┈┈┈┈┈┈

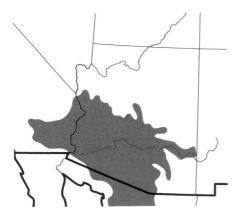

Palo verdes are usually leafless, except for a short time in the spring.

BLUE PALO VERDE
Parkinsonia florida

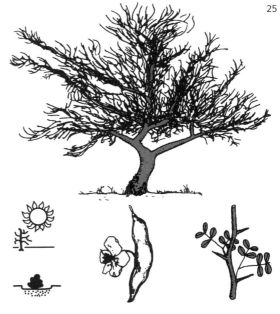

If there are single spines curved like hooks scattered along the twig, go to ·········· **>** below

If the spines are straight and grow in pairs, go to ·· **>** next page

If the trunk bark is gray and scaly, it is ············· **CATCLAW ACACIA**
Senegalia greggii

If the trunk bark is light brown with whitish lines running up and down, it is ········ **> SOUTHWESTERN CORALBEAN**
Erythrina flabelliformis

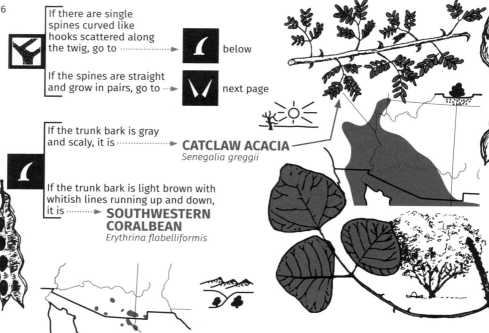

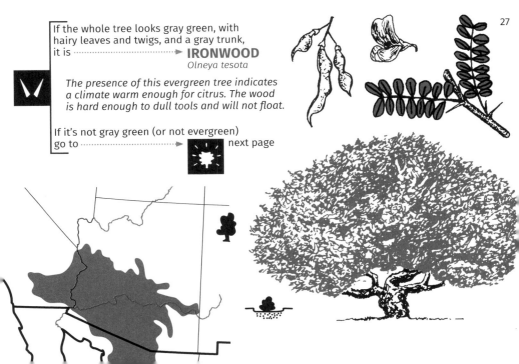

If the whole tree looks gray green, with
hairy leaves and twigs, and a gray trunk,
it is ·····························▶ **IRONWOOD**
Olneya tesota

*The presence of this evergreen tree indicates
a climate warm enough for citrus. The wood
is hard enough to dull tools and will not float.*

If it's not gray green (or not evergreen)
go to ·····························▶ next page

If there is a single leaflet at the tip of the compound leaf, or if there are dark-brown or reddish spines, it is

NEW MEXICO LOCUST
Robinia neomexicana

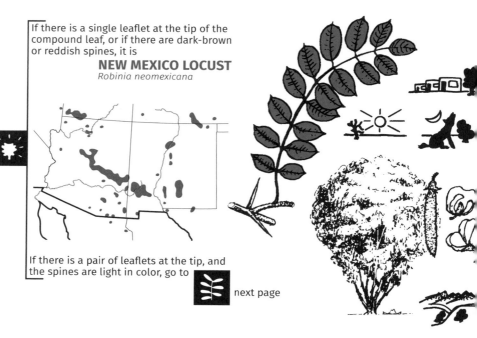

If there is a pair of leaflets at the tip, and the spines are light in color, go to

next page

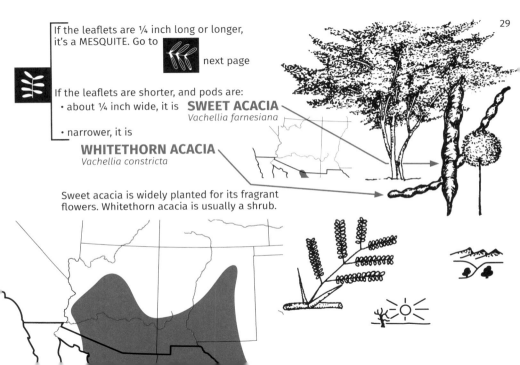

If the leaflets are ¼ inch long or longer, it's a MESQUITE. Go to next page

If the leaflets are shorter, and pods are:
- about ¼ inch wide, it is **SWEET ACACIA**
  Vachellia farnesiana

- narrower, it is

WHITETHORN ACACIA
Vachellia constricta

Sweet acacia is widely planted for its fragrant flowers. Whitethorn acacia is usually a shrub.

If the pods are twisted and screwlike, and the spines are whitish, it is ········▶ **SCREWBEAN MESQUITE**
Prosopis pubescens

If the pods are long and bean-like, go to next page

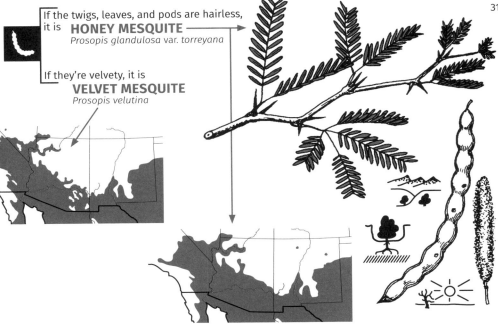

If the twigs, leaves, and pods are hairless, it is **HONEY MESQUITE**
Prosopis glandulosa var. torreyana

If they're velvety, it is **VELVET MESQUITE**
Prosopis velutina

If the leaves are tiny and scale-like, held close against the twig, go to below

If they're not scale-like, go to page 35

If crushed foliage smells resinous, it's a JUNIPER. Go to ⸺⸺⸺▶ next page

If it's not resinous, it is ⸺⸺▶ **FRENCH TAMARISK SALTCEDAR**
Tamarix gallica

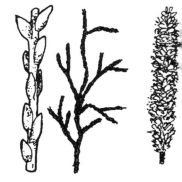

Tamarisk is usually shrub-shaped, with several long branches rising from the base. Narrow clusters of pink flowers bloom March to August. The first seeds of this Mediterranean tree probably came to America in hay for Spanish horses. It's widely naturalized along rivers, drainage ditches, and even enduring alkali flats.

INVASIVE

If the trunk bark is deeply furrowed and checkered into squarish plates, it is ·········▶ **ALLIGATOR JUNIPER**
Juniperus deppeana

If the trunk bark is stringy and fibrous, go to next page

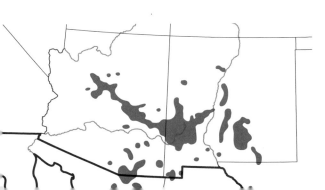

34

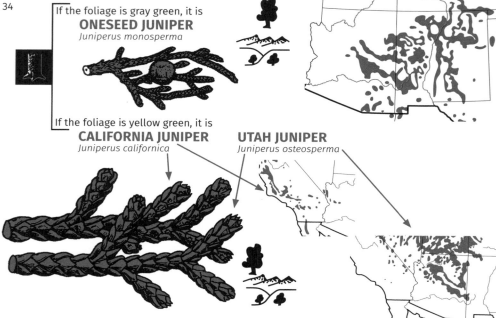

If the foliage is gray green, it is
ONESEED JUNIPER
Juniperus monosperma

If the foliage is yellow green, it is
CALIFORNIA JUNIPER
Juniperus californica

UTAH JUNIPER
Juniperus osteosperma

If the leaf surface is about as wide as it is long; either round, triangular, star-shaped, or heart-shaped; with a leaf stem an inch or more long, go to below

If the leaves are not like that, go to page 41

If the leaf is triangular with small, rounded teeth, it's a COTTONWOOD. Go to next page

Cottonwood flowers are borne in drooping catkins. The pollen-bearing catkins are more brightly colored and compact than the seed-bearing ones, which are on separate trees.

If the leaves are not triangular, go to page 38

36

If you can find seed capsules on stalks longer than ½ inch, or if buds on the twigs are slightly hairy, it is ⋯⋯⋯⋯⋯⋯► **RIO GRANDE COTTONWOOD**
Populus deltoides ssp. wislizeni

If the stalks of seed capsules are shorter; or if the buds are without hair, it is ⋯⋯⋯⋯⋯⋯► **FREMONT'S COTTONWOOD** -
Populus fremontii

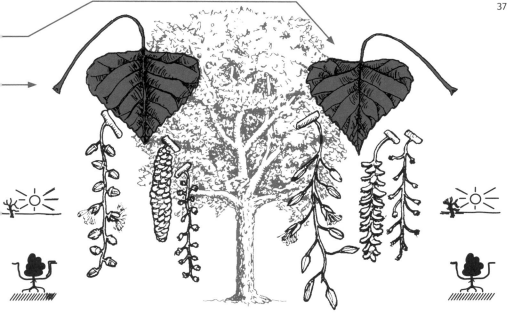

38

If the leaves are star-shaped, it is either ·······▸ **CALIFORNIA SYCAMORE**
Platanus racemosa

or

ARIZONA SYCAMORE
Platanus wrightii

If the leaves are not
star-shaped, go to page 40

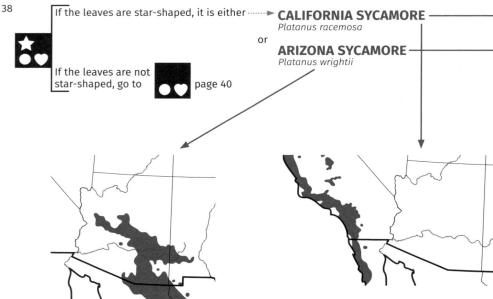

The young white branches later flake off in brown patches, eventually becoming dark gray with thick plates. The canopy is hung with small greenish balls of clustered flowers in March and April, and with brown seed balls later. Sycamores may make displaced Easterners homesick.

If the leaf is thin and round with no teeth along the margin, it is **CALIFORNIA REDBUD**
Cercis occidentalis

Redbud trees are covered with pink sweet pea–shaped flowers in spring. Later, there are flat, thin pods.

If the leaf is deeply indented, and saw-toothed along the thick, colorful margin, it is ·······························▶ **CASTORBEAN**
Ricinus communis

The long leaf stalk is hollow. The spiny seed capsule splits open, showing three extremely poisonous seeds. **Avoid contact.**

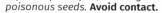

INVASIVE

If the leaves are compound, composed of three or more leaflets like this:

go to below

There's a bud on the twig at the base of a leaf, but not at the base of a leaflet.

If the leaves are not made up of leaflets, go to ·····➤ below

If the leaves (but not necessarily the leaflets) come out opposite each other, paired, along the twig, go to ···········➤ next page

If the leaves come out alternately along the twig, not in pairs, go to ···········➤ page 44

If the leaf is long and narrow (more than three times as long as wide), go to ···········➤ page 50

If it's wider than that, go to ···········➤ page 46

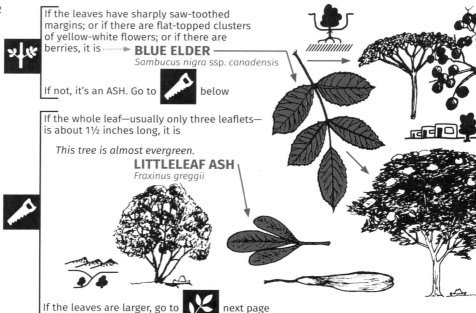

If the leaves have sharply saw-toothed margins; or if there are flat-topped clusters of yellow-white flowers; or if there are berries, it is ········▶ **BLUE ELDER**
Sambucus nigra ssp. *canadensis*

If not, it's an ASH. Go to ▢ below

If the whole leaf—usually only three leaflets—is about 1½ inches long, it is

This tree is almost evergreen.

LITTLELEAF ASH
Fraxinus greggii

If the leaves are larger, go to ▢ next page

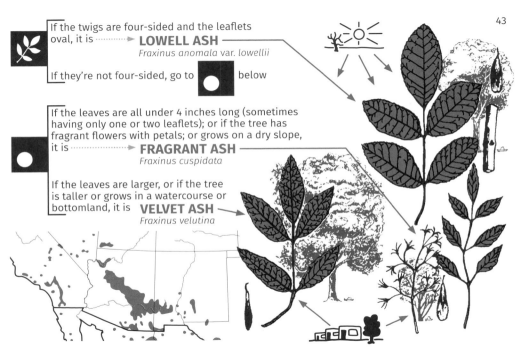

43

If the twigs are four-sided and the leaflets oval, it is ··········→ **LOWELL ASH**
Fraxinus anomala var. *lowellii*

If they're not four-sided, go to ⬤ below

If the leaves are all under 4 inches long (sometimes having only one or two leaflets); or if the tree has fragrant flowers with petals; or grows on a dry slope, it is ··········→ **FRAGRANT ASH**
Fraxinus cuspidata

If the leaves are larger, or if the tree is taller or grows in a watercourse or bottomland, it is **VELVET ASH**
Fraxinus velutina

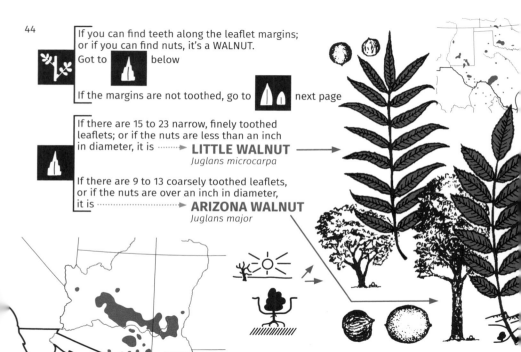

If you can find teeth along the leaflet margins; or if you can find nuts, it's a WALNUT.

Got to below

If the margins are not toothed, go to next page

If there are 15 to 23 narrow, finely toothed leaflets; or if the nuts are less than an inch in diameter, it is ·······► **LITTLE WALNUT**
Juglans microcarpa

If there are 9 to 13 coarsely toothed leaflets, or if the nuts are over an inch in diameter, it is ·······························► **ARIZONA WALNUT**
Juglans major

If the leaflets are about ¼ inch long, and the branches and trunk look thick and swollen, it is **ELEPHANT TREE**
Bursera microphylla

The tree is leafless, except after rain.

If the leaflets are larger, it is
WESTERN SOAPBERRY
WILD CHINA-TREE
Sapindus saponaria var. *drummondii*

Flowers are borne in long clusters, May to August. Fruits are yellow, berrylike, and translucent.

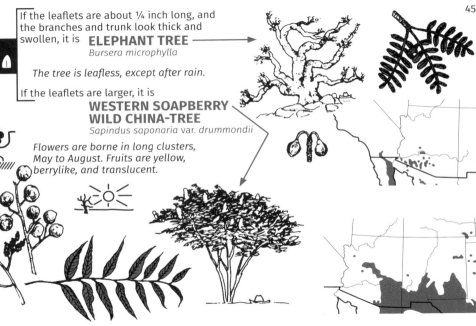

If the leaf margin is:

- stiff, with spiny points, go to next page

- saw-toothed, go to page 48

- smooth, go to below

If the leaf stem is about as long as the leaf blade, it is **TREE TOBACCO**
Nicotiana glauca

For most of the year there are tubular, yellow, fragrant flowers. The tree is native to South America but naturalized in the southwestern US.

If the leaf stems are shorter, go to page 49

INVASIVE

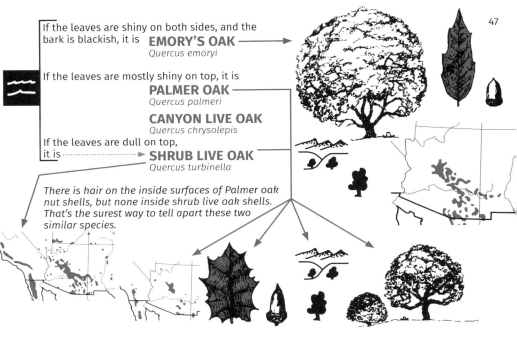

If the leaves are shiny on both sides, and the bark is blackish, it is **EMORY'S OAK**
Quercus emoryi

If the leaves are mostly shiny on top, it is

PALMER OAK
Quercus palmeri

CANYON LIVE OAK
Quercus chrysolepis

If the leaves are dull on top, it is ⟶ **SHRUB LIVE OAK**
Quercus turbinella

There is hair on the inside surfaces of Palmer oak nut shells, but none inside shrub live oak shells. That's the surest way to tell apart these two similar species.

48

If all leaves have a saw-toothed margin,
and some of them have lobes, it is
TEXAS MULBERRY
Morus microphylla

If the leaves are lopsided, usually without
teeth, it is ·········► **NETLEAF HACKBERRY**
Celtis reticulata

*There are warts on the bark, galls on the
leaves, and often tangles of dwarfed twigs
caused by a gall insect.*

If the leaf tips are rounded, it is **MEXICAN BLUE OAK**
Quercus oblongifolia

If they're pointed, it is
NETLEAF HACKBERRY
Celtis reticulata

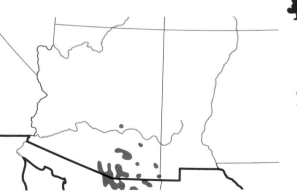

If the leaves are ¼ inch wide and over 3 inches long, it is **DESERT WILLOW**
Chilopsis linearis

If not, go to next page

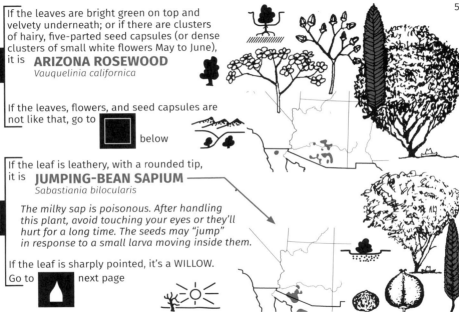

If the leaves are bright green on top and velvety underneath; or if there are clusters of hairy, five-parted seed capsules (or dense clusters of small white flowers May to June), it is **ARIZONA ROSEWOOD**
Vauquelinia californica

If the leaves, flowers, and seed capsules are not like that, go to [■] below

If the leaf is leathery, with a rounded tip, it is **JUMPING-BEAN SAPIUM**
Sabastiania bilocularis

The milky sap is poisonous. After handling this plant, avoid touching your eyes or they'll hurt for a long time. The seeds may "jump" in response to a small larva moving inside them.

If the leaf is sharply pointed, it's a WILLOW.
Go to [▲] next page

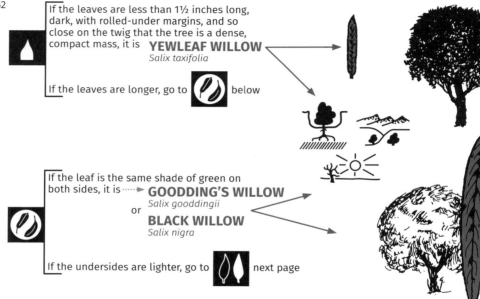

If the leaves are less than 1½ inches long, dark, with rolled-under margins, and so close on the twig that the tree is a dense, compact mass, it is **YEWLEAF WILLOW**
Salix taxifolia

If the leaves are longer, go to ⬤ below

If the leaf is the same shade of green on both sides, it is ·····▶ **GOODDING'S WILLOW**
Salix gooddingii
or
BLACK WILLOW
Salix nigra

If the undersides are lighter, go to next page

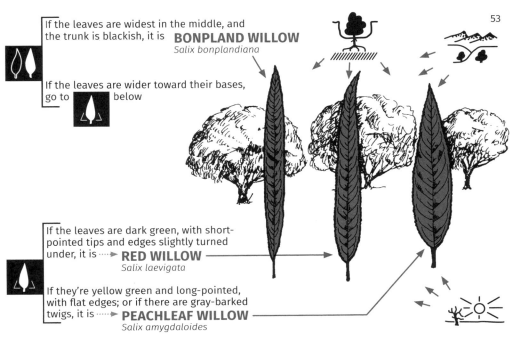

53

If the leaves are widest in the middle, and the trunk is blackish, it is **BONPLAND WILLOW**
Salix bonplandiana

If the leaves are wider toward their bases, go to below

If the leaves are dark green, with short-pointed tips and edges slightly turned under, it is ·····► **RED WILLOW**
Salix laevigata

If they're yellow green and long-pointed, with flat edges; or if there are gray-barked twigs, it is ·····► **PEACHLEAF WILLOW**
Salix amygdaloides

54

If the tree trunk is a single column topped by a cluster of leaves, go to ·······> next page

If the tree has branches, go to ·······> page 56

With abundant artificial water, almost any kind of tree will grow in a desert climate. Only a few of the more commonly cultivated species are shown here.

55

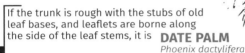

If the trunk is rough with the stubs of old
leaf bases, and leaflets are borne along
the side of the leaf stems, it is **DATE PALM**
Phoenix dactylifera

Date palms were brought from northern Africa.

If the trunk is smoother, and the leaves are
fan-like, it is **CALIFORNIA FAN PALM**
Washingtonia filifera

*Trunks of fan palms growing naturally in
the Colorado Desert often have a skirt of
old leaves. It's trimmed on street trees.*

INVASIVE

If the tree is dark green with scale-like leaves or needle-like foliage, go to below

If there are ordinary leaves, go to next page

If the foliage is feathery, with branches that look like pine needles, except that they're jointed, it is **AUSTRALIAN PINE BEEFWOOD**
Casuarina equisetifolia

This Australian tree has cone-like fruits.

If the foliage is not feathery, go to next page

INVASIVE

If there are glossy, oval leaves with winged stems, it is

ORANGE, GRAPEFRUIT, OR LEMON
Citrus sp.

These compact, evergreen trees originated in Asia. They have fragrant fruit and flowers present at the same time.

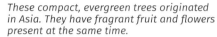

If the leaves are not glossy and oval, go to next page

If the branch tips are bluish, it is

ARIZONA CYPRESS
Cupressus arizonica var. *arizonica*

If the tree is columnar, compact, tapering, and dark green, it is **ITALIAN CYPRESS**
Cupressus sempervirens

If the leaves are long, dull green on both sides, sharply pointed, curved, and fragrant, it is ·····································► **BLUE GUM**
Eucalyptus globulus

This widely planted Australian tree sheds bark and flower capsules. Neat people prefer other species of Eucalyptus.

If the leaflets have many divisions into leaflets or lobes, go to below

If the leaves are fernlike, with rolled-under margins, silky on the undersides, it is
SILKY OAK
Grevillea robusta

This Australian tree has orange flowers and small pods.

If there are separate leaflets, go to next page

59

If the foliage is feathery and smells spicy,
it is ·······▶ **PERUVIAN PEPPERTREE**
Schinus molle

*This Peruvian tree bears long clusters
of rosy, beadlike fruit (not the pepper
Columbus sought).*

If the foliage is coarse, foul-smelling; and
the tree has thick twigs and few branches,
it is ·······▶ **TREE OF HEAVEN**
Ailanthus altissima

*This tree, which is native to Asia, has
followed people. Unfortunately, it's
now considered an invasive species.*

INDEX

Other books in the pocket-size *Finder* series:

FOR US AND CANADA EAST OF THE ROCKIES
Berry Finder native plants with fleshy fruits
Bird Finder frequently seen birds
Bird Nest Finder aboveground nests
Fern Finder native ferns of the Midwest and Northeast
Flower Finder spring wildflowers and flower families
Life on Intertidal Rocks organisms of the North Atlantic Coast
Scat Finder mammal scat
Track Finder mammal tracks and footprints
Tree Finder native and common introduced trees
Winter Tree Finder leafless winter trees
Winter Weed Finder dry plants in winter

FOR THE PACIFIC COAST
Pacific Coast Bird Finder frequently seen birds
Pacific Coast Fish Finder marine fish of the Pacific Coast
Pacific Coast Mammal Finder mammals, their tracks, skulls, and other signs

FOR THE PACIFIC COAST (continued)
Pacific Coast Tree Finder native trees, from Sitka to San Diego
Pacific Intertidal Life organisms of the Pacific Coast
Redwood Region Flower Finder wildflowers of the coastal fog belt of CA

FOR ROCKY MOUNTAIN AND DESERT STATE
Rocky Mountain Flower Finder wildflowers below tree line
Rocky Mountain Mammal Finder mammals, their track skulls, and other signs
Rocky Mountain Tree Finder native Rocky Mountain tr

FOR STARGAZERS
Constellation Finder patterns in the night sky and star stories

FOR FORAGERS
Mushroom Finder fungi of North America

NATURE STUDY GUIDES are published by AdventureKEEN, 2204 1st Ave. S., Suite 102, Birmingham, AL 35233; 800-678-7(
naturestudy.com. See shop.adventurewithkeen.com for our full line of nature and outdoor activity guides by ADVENT
PUBLICATIONS, MENASHA RIDGE PRESS, and WILDERNESS PRESS, including many guides for birding, wildflowers, ro
and trees, plus regional and national parks, hiking, camping, backpacking, and more.